A Guide to MLA Documentation

with an Appendix on APA Style

Sixth Edition

Joseph F. Trimmer

Ball State University

Houghton Mifflin Company   Boston   New York

Executive Editor: Suzanne Phelps Weir
Senior Development Editor: Sarah Helyar Smith
Senior Project Editor: Rosemary Winfield
Production/Design Coordinator: Bethany Schlegel
Senior Manufacturing Coordinator: Florence Cadran
Marketing Manager: Cindy Graff Cohen

Cover photograph © Anton Grassl Photography, www.antongrassl.com

Acknowledgments

This guide in part summarizes the documentation style of the Modern Language Association of America as it appears in Joseph Gibaldi, *MLA Handbook for Writers of Research Papers,* 6th ed. (New York: MLA, 2003); and in Joseph Gibaldi, *MLA Style Manual and Guide to Scholarly Publishing,* 2d ed. (New York: MLA, 1998); and on the MLA Web site (http://www.mla.org). This guide is not a work of the Modern Language Association of America, however, and bears no endorsement from the association. For a fuller presentation of many of the topics covered in this guide, readers should consult the resources listed above.

Printed in the U.S.A.
ISBN: 0-618-33805-5
Library of Congress Catalog Card Number:

123456789-CRS-07 06 05 04 03

Contents

This booklet explains the style recommended by the Modern Language Association (MLA) for documenting sources in research papers. It also analyzes some of the implications of MLA style for your research and composing. More detailed information is given in the MLA Handbook and the MLA Style Manual.[1]

MLA style has three major features. First, all sources cited in a paper are listed in a section entitled **Works Cited**, which is located at the end of the paper. Second, material borrowed from another source is documented within the text by a brief parenthetical reference that directs readers to the full citation in the list of works cited. Third, numbered footnotes or endnotes are used to present two types of supplementary information: (1) commentary or explanation that the text cannot accommodate and (2) bibliographical notes that contain several source citations.

1. Preparing the List of Works Cited

In a research paper that follows MLA style, the list of works cited is the only place where readers will find complete information about the sources you have cited. For that reason, your list must be thorough and accurate.

The list of works cited appears at the end of your paper and, as its title suggests, lists only the works you have cited in your paper. Occasionally, your instructor may ask you to prepare a list of works consulted. That list would include not only the sources you cite but also the sources you consulted as you conducted your research. In either case, MLA prefers Works Cited or Works Consulted to the more limited heading Bibliography (literally, "description of books") because those headings are more likely to accommodate the variety of sources—articles, films, Internet sources—that writers may cite in a research paper.

To prepare the list of works cited, follow these general guidelines:

1. Paginate the Works Cited section as a continuation of your text. If the conclusion of your paper appears on page 8, begin your list on page 9 (unless there is an intervening page of endnotes).

[1]Joseph Gibaldi, *MLA Handbook for Writers of Research Papers,* 6th ed. (New York: MLA, 2003).
Joseph Gibaldi, *MLA Style Manual and Guide to Scholarly Publishing,* 2d ed. (New York: MLA, 1998).

2. Double-space between successive lines of an entry and between entries.

3. Begin the first line of an entry flush left, and indent successive lines one-half inch or five spaces.

4. List entries in alphabetical order according to the last name of the author.

5. If you are listing more than one work by the same author, alphabetize the works according to title (excluding the articles *a, an,* and *the*). Instead of repeating the author's name, type *three* hyphens and a period, and then give the title.

6. Underline the titles of works published as independent units: books, plays, long poems, pamphlets, periodicals, films. Do not underline article titles.

7. Although you do not need to underline the spaces between words, a continuous line is easier to type and guarantees that all features of the title are underlined. Type a continuous line under titles unless you are instructed to do otherwise.

8. If you are citing a book whose title includes the title of another book, underline the main title, but do not underline the other title (for example, A Casebook on Ralph Ellison's Invisible Man).

9. Use quotation marks to indicate titles of short works, such as articles, that appear in larger works (for example, "Minutes of Glory." African Short Stories). Also use quotation marks for song titles and for titles of unpublished works, including dissertations, lectures, and speeches.

10. Use arabic numerals except with names of monarchs (Elizabeth II) and except for the preliminary pages of a work (ii–xix), which are traditionally numbered with roman numerals.

11. Use lowercase abbreviations to identify the parts of a work (for example, *vol.* for *volume*), a named translator (*trans.*), and a named editor (*ed.*). However, when these designations follow a period, they should be capitalized (for example, Woolf, Virginia. A Writer's Diary. Ed. Leonard Woolf).

12. Whenever possible, use appropriate shortened forms for the publisher's name (*Random* instead of *Random House*). See the list of abbreviations beginning on page 36.

13. Separate author, title, and publication information with a period followed by one space.

14. Use a colon and one space to separate the volume number and year of a periodical from the page numbers (for example, Trimmer, Joseph. "Memoryscape: Jean Shepherd's Midwest." Old Northwest 2 (1976): 357–69).

15. Treat inclusive page numbers in text citations and in the list of works cited as follows: 67–68, 102–03, 237–42, 389–421.

In addition to these guidelines, MLA recommends procedures for documenting an extensive variety of sources, including electronic sources and non-print materials such as films and television programs. The following models illustrate sources most commonly cited.

Sample Entries: Books

When citing books, provide the following general categories of information:

Author's last name, first name. Book title. Additional information. City of publication: Publisher, publication date.

Entries illustrating variations on this basic format appear below and are numbered to facilitate reference.

A Book by One Author

1. Light, Richard J. Making the Most of College: Students Speak Their Minds. Cambridge: Harvard UP, 2001.

Two or More Books by the Same Author

2. Garreau, Joel. Edge City: Life on the New Frontier. New York: Doubleday, 1991.

3. - - -. The Nine Nations of North America. Boston: Houghton, 1981.

A Book by Two or Three Authors

4. Vare, Ethlie Ann, and Greg Ptacek. Mothers of Invention: From the Bra to the Bomb: Forgotten Women and Their Unforgettable Ideas. New York: Morrow, 1988.

5. Atwan, Robert, Donald McQuade, and John W. Wright. Edsels, Luckies, and Frigidaires: Advertising the American Way. New York: Dell, 1979.

A Book by Four or More Authors

6. Belenky, Mary Field, et al. Women's Ways of Knowing: The Development of
   Self, Voice, and Mind. New York: Basic, 1986.

A Book by a Corporate Author

7. National Geographic Society. Cradle and Crucible: History and Faith in the
   Middle East. Washington: National Geographic, 2002.

A Book by an Anonymous Author

8. Literary Market Place: The Dictionary of American Book Publishing. 1998
   ed. New York: Bowker, 1997.

A Book with an Editor

9. Jackson, Kenneth T. The Encyclopedia of New York City. New Haven: Yale
   UP, 1995.

A Book with an Author and an Editor

10. Toomer, Jean. Cane. Ed. Darwin T. Turner. New York: Norton, 1988.

A Book with a Publisher's Imprint

11. Hillenbrand, Laura. Seabiscuit: An American Legend. New York: Ballantine-
    Random, 2001.

An Anthology or Compilation

12. Valdez, Luis, and Stan Steiner, eds. Aztlan: An Anthology of Mexican
    American Literature. New York: Vintage-Knopf, 1972.

A Work in an Anthology

13. Silko, Leslie Marmon. "The Man to Send Rain Clouds." <u>Imagining America:
    Stories from the Promised Land</u>. Ed. Wesley Brown and Amy Ling.
    New York: Persea, 1991. 191–95.

An Introduction, Preface, Foreword, or Afterword

14. Bernstein, Carl. Afterword. <u>Muckraking</u>. By Jessica Mitford. New York:
    Vintage-Random, 1979. 275–77.

A Multivolume Work

15. Blotner, Joseph. <u>Faulkner: A Biography</u>. 2 vols. New York: Random,
    1974.

An Edition Other Than the First

16. Chaucer, Geoffrey. <u>The Riverside Chaucer</u>. Ed. Larry D. Benson. 3rd ed.
    Boston: Houghton, 1987.

A Book in a Series

17. McClave, Heather, ed. <u>Women Writers of the Short Story</u>. Twentieth Century
    Views. Englewood Cliffs: Spectrum-Prentice, 1980.

A Republished Book

18. Malamud, Bernard. <u>The Natural</u>. 1952. New York: Avon, 1980.

A Signed Article in a Reference Book

19. Tobias, Richard. "Thurber, James." <u>Encyclopedia Americana</u>.
    2002 ed.

An Unsigned Article in a Reference Book

20. "Tharp, Twyla." Who's Who of American Women. 17th ed. 1991–92.

A Government Document

21. United States. Cong. House. Committee on the Judiciary. Immigration and
        Nationality Act with Amendments and Notes on Related Laws. 7th ed.
        Washington: GPO, 1980.

Published Proceedings of a Conference

22. Griggs, John, ed. AIDS: Public Policy Dimensions. Proc. of a conference.
        16–17 Jan. 1986. New York: United Hospital Fund of New York, 1987.

A Translation

23. Giroud, Françoise. Marie Curie: A Life. Trans. Lydia Davis. New York:
        Holmes, 1986.

A Book with a Title in Its Title

24. Habich, Robert D. Transcendentalism and the Western Messenger: A History
        of the Magazine and Its Contributors, 1835–1841. Rutherford:
        Fairleigh Dickinson UP, 1985.

A Book Published Before 1900

25. Field, Kate. The History of Bell's Telephone. London, 1878.

An Unpublished Dissertation

26. Geissinger, Shirley Burry. "Openness versus Secrecy in Adoptive
        Parenthood." Diss. U of North Carolina at Greensboro, 1984.

A Published Dissertation

27. Ames, Barbara Edwards. <u>Dreams and Painting: A Case Study of the Relationship between an Artist's Dreams and Painting</u>. Diss. U of Virginia, 1978. Ann Arbor: UMI, 1979. 7928021.

Sample Entries: Articles in Periodicals

When citing articles in periodicals, provide the following general categories of information:

Author's last name, first name. "Article title." <u>Periodical title</u> Date: inclusive pages.

Entries illustrating variations on this basic format appear below and are numbered to facilitate reference.

A Signed Article from a Daily Newspaper

28. Barringer, Felicity. "Where Many Elderly Live, Signs of the Future." <u>New York Times</u> 7 Mar. 1993, nat. ed., sec. 1: 12.

An Unsigned Article from a Daily Newspaper

29. "Infant Mortality Down; Race Disparity Widens." <u>Washington Post</u> 12 Mar. 1993: A12.

An Article from a Monthly or Bimonthly Magazine

30. Wills, Garry. "The Words That Remade America: Lincoln at Gettysburg." <u>Atlantic</u> June 1992: 57–79.

An Article from a Weekly or Biweekly Magazine

31. Sedaris, David. "Who's the Chef?" <u>New Yorker</u> 10 March 2003: 40–41.

An Article in a Journal with Continuous Pagination

32. Hesse, Douglas. "The Place of Creative Nonfiction." College English 65
    (2003): 237–41.

An Article in a Journal That Numbers Pages in Each Issue Separately

33. Seely, Bruce. "The Saga of American Infrastructure: A Republic Bound
    Together." Wilson Quarterly 17.1 (1993): 19–39.

An Editorial

34. "A Question of Medical Sight." Editorial. Plain Dealer [Cleveland, OH] 11
    Mar. 1993: 6B.

A Review

35. Morson, Gary Soul. "Coping with Utopia." Soviet Civilization: A Rev. of
    Cultural History, by Andrei Sinyavsky. American Scholar 61 (1992):
    132–38.

An Article Whose Title Contains a Quotation or a Title Within Quotation Marks

36. DeCuir, Andre L. "Italy, England and the Female Artist in George Eliot's
    'Mr. Gilfil's Love-Story.'" Studies in Short Fiction 29 (1992): 67–75.

An Abstract from *Dissertation Abstracts* or *Dissertation Abstracts International*

37. Creek, Mardena Bridges. "Myth, Wound, Accommodation: American
    Literary Responses to the War in Vietnam." DAI 43 (1982): 3539A.
    Ball State U.

Sample Entries: CD-ROMs

When citing information from CD-ROMs, provide the following general categories of information:

Author's last name, first name (if available). "Article title of printed source or
   printed analogue." Periodical title of printed source or printed analogue
   Date: inclusive pages. Title of database. CD-ROM. Name of vendor or computer service. Electronic publication date or date of access.

Entries illustrating variations on this basic format appear below and are numbered to facilitate reference.

CD-ROM: Periodical Publication with Printed Source or Printed Analogue

38. West, Cornel. "The Dilemma of the Black Intellectual." Critical Quarterly
      29 (1987): 39–52. MLA International Bibliography. CD-ROM. Silver
      Platter. Feb. 1995.

CD-ROM: Nonperiodical Publication

39. Cinemania 97. CD-ROM. Redmond: Microsoft, 1996.

CD-ROM: A Work in More Than One Electronic Medium

40. Mozart. CD-ROM. Laser disk. Union City, CA: Ebook, 1992.

Sample Entries: Internet and Web Sources

When citing information from Internet and World Wide Web sources, provide the following general categories of information:

Author's last name, first name. "Article title" or Book title. Publication
   information for any printed version. Or subject line of forum or discussion
   group. Indication of online posting or home page. Title of electronic journal.

> Date of electronic publication. Page numbers or the numbers of paragraphs or sections. Name of institution or organization sponsoring Web site. Date of access to the source <URL>.

Enclose the URL in angle brackets. For lengthy or complex URLs, give enough information about the path so a reader can locate the exact page you are referring to from the search page of the site or the database. If you need to break a URL at the end of a line, do so only after a slash and do not add any hyphens or punctuation that are not in the original URL.

The speed of change in the electronic world means that particular features for citing Internet and Web sources are constantly evolving. The best way to confirm the accuracy of your citations is to check the MLA Web site (<http://www.mla.org>).

Entries illustrating variations on the basic format appear below and are numbered to facilitate reference.

A Professional Site

41. MLA Style. 4 April 2002. Modern Language Association of America. 26 Mar. 2003 <http://www.mla.org>.

A Personal Site

42. Hawisher, Gail. Home page. University of Illinois Urbana-Champaign. 26 Mar. 2003 <http://www.english.uiuc.edu/facpages/Hawisher.htm>.

A Book

43. Conrad, Joseph. Lord Jim. London: Blackwood, 1900. Oxford Text Archive. 12 July 1993. Oxford University Computing Services. 20 Feb. 1998 <ftp://ota.ox.ac.uk/pub/ota/public/english/conrad/lordjim.1824>.

A Poem

44. Roethke, Theodore. "My Papa's Waltz," Favorite Poem Project. <http://www.favoritepoem.org/poems/roethke/waltz.html>.

An Article in a Reference Database

45. "Women in American History." <u>Britannica Online</u> Vers. 98.1.1. Nov. 1997.

    Encyclopedia Britannica. 10 Mar. 1998

    <http://www.britannica.com>.

An Article in a Journal

46. Bieder, Robert A. "The Representation of Indian Bodies in Nineteenth-

    Century American Anthropology." <u>American Indian Quarterly</u>

    20.2 (1996). 28 Mar. 1998

    <http://www.uoknor.edu/aiq/aiq202.html#beider>.

An Article in a Magazine

47. Levine, Judith. "I Surf, Therefore I Am." <u>Salon</u> 29 July 1997. 9 Dec. 1997

    <http://www.salonmagazine.com/July97/mothers/surfing.970729.html>.

A Review

48. Roth, Martha. "A Tantalizing Remoteness." Rev. of <u>Jane Austen: A</u>

    <u>Biography</u> by Claire Tomalin. <u>Hungry Mind Review</u> Winter 1997.

    10 Mar. 1998

    <http://www.bookwire.com/HMR/nonfiction/read.review$5376>.

A Posting to a Discussion Group

49. Inman, James. "Re: Technologist." Online posting. 24 Sept. 1997. Alliance

    for Computers in Writing. 27 Mar. 1998

    <acw-l@unicorn.acs.ttu.edu>.

A Personal E-mail Message

50. Penning, Sarah. "Mentor Advice." E-mail to Rai Peterson. 6 May 1995.

Sample Entries: Other Sources

Films; Radio and Television Programs

51. <u>Chicago</u>. Dir. Rob Marshall. With Renée Zellweger, Catherine Zeta-Jones, Richard Gere. Miramax, 2002.

52. "If God Ever Listened: A Portrait of Alice Walker." <u>Horizons</u>. Prod. Jane Rosenthal. NPR. WBST, Muncie. 3 Mar. 1984.

53. "The Hero's Adventure." <u>Moyers: Joseph Campbell and the Power of Myth</u>. Prod. Catherine Tatge. PBS. WNET, New York. 23 May 1988.

Performances

54. <u>The Producers</u>. By Mel Brooks. Dir. Susan Stroman. With Nathan Lane and Matthew Broderick. St. James Theater. 8 October 2002.

55. Ozawa, Seiji, cond. Boston Symphony Orch. Concert. Symphony Hall, Boston. 30 Sept. 1988.

Recordings

If you are not referring to an audio recording on a CD, then add the medium before the manufacturer.

56. Mozart, Wolfgang A. <u>Cosi Fan Tutte</u>. Record. With Kiri Te Kanawa, Frederica von Stade, David Rendall, and Philippe Huttenlocher. Cond. Alain Lombard. Strasbourg Philharmonic Orch. LP. RCA, 1978.

57. Jones, Norah. <u>Come Away with Me</u>. Blue Note, 2002.

Works of Art

58. Botticelli, Sandro. <u>Giuliano de' Medici</u>. Samuel H. Kress Collection. National Gallery of Art, Washington.

59. Rodin, Auguste. <u>The Gates of Hell</u>. Rodin Museum, Paris.

Maps and Charts

60. <u>Sonoma and Napa Counties</u>. Map. San Francisco: California State Automobile
    Assn., 1984.

Cartoons and Advertisements

61. Addams, Charles. Cartoon. <u>New Yorker</u> 22 Feb. 1988: 33.

62. Air France. "The Fine Art of Flying." Advertisement. <u>Travel and Leisure</u>
    May 1988: 9.

Published and Unpublished Letters

63. Fitzgerald, F. Scott. "To Ernest Hemingway." 1 June 1934. <u>The Letters of
    F. Scott Fitzgerald</u>. Ed. Andrew Turnbull. New York: Scribner's, 1963.
    308–10.

64. Stowe, Harriet Beecher. Letter to George Eliot. 25 May 1869. Berg
    Collection. New York: New York Public Library.

Interviews

65. Ellison, Ralph. "Indivisible Man." Interview. By James Alan McPherson.
    <u>Atlantic</u> Dec. 1970: 45–60.

66. Diamond, Carol. Telephone interview. 27 Dec. 1988.

Lectures, Speeches, and Addresses

67. Russo, Michael. "A Painter Speaks His Mind." Museum of Fine Arts. Boston,
    5 Aug. 1984.

68. Baker, Houston A., Jr. "The Presidential Address." MLA Convention. New
    York, 28 Dec. 1992.

2. Documenting Sources

The purpose of a parenthetical reference is to document a source briefly, clearly, and accurately. Brevity can be accomplished in three ways.

1. Cite the author's last name and the page number(s) of the source in parentheses.

> One historian argues that since the invention of television "our politics, religion, news, athletics, education and commerce have been transformed into congenial adjuncts of show business, largely without protest or even much popular notice" (Postman 3–4).

2. Use the author's last name in your sentence, and place only the page number(s) of the source in parentheses.

> Postman points out that since the invention of television "our politics, religion, news, athletics, education and commerce have been transformed into congenial adjuncts of show business, largely without protest or even much popular notice" (3–4).

3. Give the author's last name in your sentence when you are citing the *entire work* rather than a *specific* section or passage, and omit any parenthetical reference.

> Postman argues that television has changed virtually every aspect of our culture into a form of show business.

Each of those in-text references is brief and clear and refers readers to a specific and complete citation listed in Works Cited. The citation looks like this:

Works Cited

Postman, Neil. <u>Amusing Ourselves to Death: Public Discourse in the Age of Show Business</u>. New York: Penguin-Viking, 1985.

Placing and Punctuating the Parenthetical Reference

To avoid clutter in sentences, MLA recommends placing the parenthetical reference at the end of the sentence but before the final period. Notice that there is no punctuation mark between the author's name and the page citation.

> In the nineteenth century, the supposed golden age of American education, "college faculties acted as disciplinary tribunals, periodically reviewing violations of rules . . ." (Graff 25).

On some occasions, you may want to place the reference within your sentence to clarify its relationship to the part of the sentence it documents. In such instances, place the reference at the end of the clause but before the necessary comma.

> Graff suggests that even though college faculties in the nineteenth century "acted as disciplinary tribunals, periodically reviewing violations of rules" (25), the myth persists that they taught in the golden age of American education.

When the reference documents a long quotation that is set off from the text, place it at the end of the passage but *after* the final period. (See page 23 for a discussion of long quotations.)

> Gerald Graff's description of the college in the nineteenth century corrects the popular myth about the golden age of American education:
>
> > College faculties acted as disciplinary tribunals, periodically reviewing violations of rules such as those requiring students to attend chapel services early every morning, to remain in their rooms for hours every day, and to avoid the snares of town. Nor were these restrictions relaxed for the many students in their late twenties or older, who lived alongside freshmen as young as fourteen. The classes themselves, conducted by the system of daily recitations, were said to have "the fearsome atmosphere of a police-station." (25)

Works Cited

Graff, Gerald. <u>Professing Literature: An Institutional History</u>. Chicago: U of

  Chicago P, 1987.

Citing Sources: Examples

Frequently, you will need to cite sources that are not as straightforward as the examples given above. In those cases, you will need to modify the standard format according to the variations illustrated below. Each example is followed by the appropriate entry that would appear in the list of works cited.

1. Citing one work by the author of two or more works

If your list of works cited contains two or more titles by the same author, place a comma after the author's last name, add a shortened version of the title of the work, and then supply the relevant page numbers. Another solution is to cite the author's last name and title in your sentence and then add the page numbers in a parenthetical reference.

Once society reaches a certain stage of industrial growth, it will shift its

energies to the production of services (Toffler, <u>Future</u> 221).

Toffler argues in <u>The Third Wave</u> that society has gone through two eras

(agricultural and industrial) and is now entering another: the information age

(26).

Works Cited

Toffler, Alvin. <u>Future Shock</u>. New York: Random, 1970.

– – –. <u>The Third Wave</u>. New York: Morrow, 1980.

2. Citing one work by an author who has the same last name as another author in your list of works cited

When your list contains sources by two or more authors with the same last name, avoid confusion by adding the initial of the author's first name in the parenthetical reference and the author's first name in your sentence. In the list of works cited, alphabetize the two authors according to first name.

Critics have often debated the usefulness of the psychological approach to literary interpretation (F. Hoffman 317).

Daniel Hoffman argues that folklore and myth provide valuable insights for the literary critic (9–15).

Works Cited

Hoffman, Daniel G. Form and Fable in American Fiction. New York: Oxford UP, 1961.

Hoffman, Frederick J. Freudianism and the Literary Mind. Baton Rouge: Louisiana State UP, 1945.

3. Citing a multivolume work

If you are citing one volume from a multivolume work, indicate in your parenthetical reference the specific volume you used.

William Faulkner's initial reluctance to travel to Stockholm to receive the Nobel Prize produced considerable consternation in the American embassy (Blotner 2: 1347).

Works Cited

Blotner, Joseph. Faulkner: A Biography. 2 vols. New York: Random, 1974.

4. Citing a work by more than one author

If you are citing a book by two or three authors, you may supply their last names in a parenthetical reference or in your sentence. To sustain the readability of your sentence if you are citing a book by four or more authors, use the first author's last name and "et al." ("and others") in a parenthetical reference or in your sentence.

Boller and Story interpret the Declaration of Independence as Thomas Jefferson's attempt to list America's grievances against England (2: 62).

Other historians view the Declaration of Independence as Jefferson's attempt to formulate the principles of America's political philosophy (Norton et al. 141).

Works Cited

Boller, Paul F., Jr., and Ronald Story. A More Perfect Union: Documents in U.S.

History. 2 vols. 5th ed. Boston: Houghton, 2000.

Norton, Mary Beth, et al. A People and a Nation: A History of the United States.

6th ed. Boston: Houghton, 2001.

5.   Citing a work by title

In the list of works cited, alphabetize works by anonymous authors according to the first main word in the title. The initial articles *a, an,* and *the* are not counted as first words. A shortened version of the title—or the title itself, if it is short—replaces the author's last name in the text citation or parenthetical reference. If you shorten the title, be sure to begin with the word that the source is alphabetized by in the list of works cited.

The recent exhibit of nineteenth-century patent models at the Cooper-Hewitt

Museum featured plans for such inventions as the Rotating Blast-Producing

Chair, an Improved Creeping-Doll, and the Life-Preserving Coffin: In Doubtful

Cases of Actual Death ("Talk").

Notice that this example follows MLA's recommendation to omit page numbers in a parenthetical reference when citing a one-page article.

Works Cited

"The Talk of the Town." New Yorker 16 July 1984: 23.

6.   Citing a work by a corporate author or government agency

If the author of your source is a corporation or a government agency, you may include the appropriate citation within parentheses (AT&T 3). It is more graceful, however, to include this information in your sentence, particularly if you are citing several corporate or government reports in one text.

AT&T's Annual Report for 2001 announced that the corporation had

reached a turning point in its history (3).

Works Cited

AT&T. Annual Report 2001. New York: AT&T, 2002.

7. Citing literary works

Because literary works—novels, plays, poems—are available in many editions, MLA recommends that you provide information in addition to page numbers, so readers using editions different from yours can locate the passage you are citing. After the page number, add a semicolon and other appropriate information, using lowercase abbreviations such as *pt., sec., ch.*

Although Flaubert sees Madame Bovary for what she is - - a silly, romantic woman - - he insists that "none of us can ever express the exact measure of his needs or his thoughts or his sorrows" and that all of us "long to make music that will melt the stars" (216; pt. 2, ch. 12).

Works Cited

Flaubert, Gustave. Madame Bovary: Patterns of Provincial Life. Trans. Francis

Steegmuller. New York: Modern Library–Random, 1957.

When citing classic verse plays and poems, omit all page numbers and document by division(s) and line(s), using periods to separate the various numbers. You can also use appropriate abbreviations to designate certain well-known works. For example, *Od.* 8.326 refers to book 8, line 326, of Homer's *Odyssey*. Do not use the abbreviation *l.* or *ll.* to indicate lines because the letters can be confused with numbers.

Also, as shown in the *Odyssey* citation given above, use arabic numerals rather than roman numerals to indicate divisions and page numbers. Some teachers still prefer to use roman numerals for documenting acts and scenes in plays (for example, *Macbeth* III.iv). If your instructor does not insist on this practice, follow MLA style and use arabic numerals (and appropriate abbreviations) to cite famous plays: *Mac.* 3.4.

8. Citing more than one work in a single parenthetical reference

If you need to include two or more works in a single parenthetical reference, document each reference according to the normal pattern, but separate each citation with a semicolon.

(Oleson 59; Trimble 85; Hylton 63)

Works Cited

Hylton, Marion Willard. "On a Trail of Pollen: Momaday's House Made of Dawn."

Critique: Studies in Modern Fiction 14.2 (1972): 60–69.

Oleson, Carole. "The Remembered Earth: Momaday's House Made of Dawn."

South Dakota Review 11 (1973): 59–78.

Trimble, Martha Scott. N. Scott Momaday. Boise State College Western Writers

Series. Boise: Boise State Col., 1973.

Although MLA style provides this procedure for documenting multiple citations within a parenthetical reference, MLA recommends citing multiple sources in a numbered bibliographic note rather than parenthetically in the text so the flow of the text is not interrupted.

3. Using Notes and Parenthetical References

In MLA style, notes (preferably endnotes) are reserved for two specific purposes.

1. To supply additional commentary on the information in the text

Thurber's reputation continued to grow until the 1950s, when he was forced to give up drawing because of his blindness.[1]

Note

[1] Thurber's older brother accidentally shot him in the eye with an arrow when they were children, causing the immediate loss of that eye. He gradually lost the sight of the other eye because of complications from the accident and a cataract.

2. To list (and perhaps evaluate) several sources or to refer readers to additional sources

The argument that American policy in Vietnam was on the whole morally justified has come under attack from many quarters.[1]

Note

[1] For a useful sampling of opinion, see Draper 32 and Nardin and Slater 437.

Notice that the sources cited in this note are documented like parenthetical references and the note itself directs readers to the complete citation in the list of works cited.

Works Cited

Draper, Theodore. "Ghosts of Vietnam." <u>Dissent</u> 26 (1979): 30–41.

Nardin, Terry, and Jerome Slater. "Vietnam Revisited." <u>World Politics</u> 33

(1981): 436–48.

As illustrated above, a note is signaled with a superscript numeral (a numeral raised above the line) typed at an appropriate place in the text (most often at the end of a sentence, after the period). The note itself, identified by a matching number followed by a space, appears at the end of the text (an endnote) or at the bottom of the page (a footnote). MLA recommends that you keep such notes to a minimum so readers are not distracted from your main point.

4. Implications for Your Research and Composing

MLA style emphasizes the importance of following the procedures for planning and writing the research paper outlined in any standard writing textbook. In particular, MLA style requires you to devote considerable attention to certain steps in your research and composing.

Compiling Source Information

Once you have located sources that you suspect will prove useful, fill out a source card or create a computer file for each item. List the source in the appropriate format (use the formats shown in the guidelines for preparing the list of works cited, pages 1–13). To guarantee that each card or file is complete and accurate, take your information directly from the source rather than from the card or online catalog or a bibliographical index. Your collection of cards or files will help you keep track of your sources throughout your research. Alphabetizing the cards or files will enable you to prepare a provisional list of works cited.

The provisional list must be in place *before* you begin writing your paper. You may expand or refine the list as you write, but to document each source in your text, you first need to know its correct citation. Thus, although Works Cited will be the last section of your paper, you must prepare it first.

Taking Notes

Note-taking demands that you read, select, interpret, and evaluate the information that will form the substance of your paper. After you return books and articles to the library, your notes will be the only record of your research. If you have taken notes carelessly, you will be in trouble when you try to use them in the body of your paper. Many students inadvertently plagiarize because they are working from inaccurate note cards or have incorrectly copied and pasted sources into their note files. (See "Avoiding Plagiarism," page 25.) As you select information from a source, use one of three methods to record it: quoting, summarizing, or paraphrasing.

Quoting Sources

Although quoting an author's text word for word is the easiest way to record information, use this method selectively and quote only the passages that deal directly with your subject in memorable language. When you copy a quotation onto a note card, place quotation marks at the beginning and the end of the passage. If you decide to omit part of the passage, use ellipsis points to indicate that you have omitted words from the original source. To indicate an omission from the middle of a sentence, use three periods (. . .), and leave a space before and after each period. For an omission at the end of a sentence, type three spaced periods following the sentence period.

To move a quotation from your notes to your paper, making it fit smoothly into the flow of your text, use one of the following methods.

1. Work the quoted passage into the syntax of your sentence.

Morrison points out that social context prevented the authors of slave narratives "from dwelling too long or too carefully on the more sordid details of their experience" (109).

2. Introduce the quoted passage with a sentence and a colon.

Commentators have tried to account for the decorum of most slave narratives by discussing social context: "popular taste discouraged the writers from dwelling too long or too carefully on the more sordid details of their experience" (Morrison 109).

3. Set off the quoted passage with an introductory sentence followed by a colon.

This method is reserved for long quotations (four or more lines of prose; three or more lines of poetry). Double-space the quotation, and indent it one inch (ten spaces) from the left margin. Because this special placement identifies the passage as a quotation, do not enclose it within quotation marks. Notice that the final period goes *before* rather than *after* the parenthetical reference. Leave one space after the final period. If the long quotation extends to two or more paragraphs, then indent the first line of these additional paragraphs one-quarter inch (three spaces).

Toni Morrison, in "The Site of Memory," explains how social context shaped slave narratives:

> No slave society in the history of the world wrote more - - or more thoughtfully - - about its own enslavement. The milieu, however, dictated the purpose and the style. The narratives are instructive, moral and obviously representative. Some of them are patterned after the sentimental novel that was in vogue at the time. But whatever the level of eloquence or the form, popular taste discouraged the writers from

dwelling too long or too carefully on the more sordid details of their experience. (109)

Summarizing and Paraphrasing Sources

Summarizing and paraphrasing an author's text are the most efficient ways to record information. The terms *summary* and *paraphrase* are often used interchangeably to describe a brief restatement of the author's ideas in your own words, but they may be used more precisely to designate different procedures. A *summary* condenses the content of a lengthy passage. When you write a summary, you reformulate the main idea and outline the main points that support it. A *paraphrase* restates the content of a short passage. When you paraphrase, you reconstruct the passage phrase by phrase, recasting the author's words in your own.

A summary or a paraphrase is intended as a complete and objective presentation of an author's ideas, so be careful not to distort the original passage by omitting major points or by adding your own opinion. Because the words of a summary or a paraphrase are yours, they are not enclosed by quotation marks. But because the ideas you are restating came from someone else, you need to cite the source in your notes and in your text. (See "Avoiding Plagiarism," page 25.)

The following examples illustrate two common methods of introducing a summary or a paraphrase into your paper.

1. Summary of a long quotation (See the Morrison quotation on page 23.)

Often, the best way to proceed is to name the author of a source in the body of your sentence and place the page numbers in parentheses. This procedure informs your reader that you are about to quote or paraphrase. It also gives you an opportunity to state the credentials of the authority you are citing.

Award-winning novelist Toni Morrison argues that although slaves wrote many powerful narratives, the context of their enslavement prevented them from telling the whole truth about their lives (109).

2. Paraphrase of a short quotation (See the fourth sentence of the Morrison quotation on page 23.)

You may decide to vary the pattern of documentation by presenting the information from a source and placing the author's name and page numbers in parentheses at the end of the sentence. This method is particularly useful if you have already established the identity of your source in a previous sentence and now want to develop the author's ideas in some detail without having to clutter your sentences with constant references to his or her name.

Slave narratives sometimes imitated the popular fiction of their era

(Morrison 109).

Works Cited

Morrison, Toni. "The Site of Memory." Inventing the Truth: The Art and Craft of

Memoir. Ed. William Zinsser. Boston: Houghton, 1987. 101–24.

Avoiding Plagiarism

Plagiarism is theft. It is using someone else's words or ideas without giving proper credit—or without giving any credit at all—to the writer of the original. Whether plagiarism is intentional or unintentional, it is a serious offense that your professor and school will deal with severely. You can avoid plagiarism by taking notes carefully, by formulating and developing your own ideas, and by using quotes responsibly to support, rather than to replace, your own work. Adhere to the advice for research and composing outlined above and demonstrated below.

The following excerpt is from Robert Hughes's *The Fatal Shore,* an account of the founding of Australia. The examples of how students tried to use this excerpt illustrate the problem of plagiarism.

Original Version

Transportation did not stop crime in England or even slow it down. The "criminal class" was not eliminated by transportation, and could not be, because transportation did not deal with the causes of crime.

Version A

Transportation did not stop crime in England or even slow it down. Criminals were not eliminated by transportation because transportation did not deal with the causes of crime.

Version A is plagiarism. Because the writer of Version A does not indicate in the text or in a parenthetical reference that the words and ideas belong to Hughes, her readers will believe the words are hers. She has stolen the words and ideas and has attempted to cover the theft by changing or omitting an occasional word.

Version B

Robert Hughes points out that transportation did not stop crime in England or even slow it down. The criminal class was not eliminated by transportation, and could not be, because transportation did not deal with the causes of crime (168).

Version B is also plagiarism, even though the writer acknowledges his source and documents the passage with a parenthetical reference. He has worked from careless notes and has misunderstood the difference between quoting and paraphrasing. He has copied the original word for word yet has supplied no quotation marks to indicate the extent of the borrowing. As written and documented, the passage masquerades as a paraphrase when in fact it is a direct quotation.

Version C

Hughes argues that transporting criminals from England to Australia "did not stop crime. . . . The 'criminal class' was not eliminated by transportation, and could not be, because transportation did not deal with the causes of crime" (168).

Version C is one satisfactory way of handling this source material. The writer has identified her source at the beginning of the sentence, letting readers know who is being quoted. She then explains the concept of transportation in her own words, placing within quotation marks the parts of the original she wants to quote and using ellipsis points to delete the parts she wants to omit. She provides a parenthetical reference to the page number in the source listed in Works Cited.

Works Cited

Hughes, Robert. The Fatal Shore. New York: Knopf, 1987.

5. Sample Outline and Research Paper

The author of the following research paper used many features of MLA style to document her paper. At her instructor's request, she first submitted a final version of her thesis and outline. Adhering to MLA style, she did not include a title page with her outline or her paper. Instead, she typed her name, her instructor's name, the course title, and the date on separate lines (double-spacing between lines) at the upper left margin. Then, after double-spacing again, she typed the title of her paper, double-spaced, and started the first line of her text. On page 1 and successive pages, she typed her last name and the page number in the upper right-hand corner, as recommended by MLA.

Blythe Rogers

English 104

Mr. Johnson

17 December 1999

Assessing Coffee's Health Problems

<u>Thesis</u>: Coffee lovers may be able to drink their coffee and keep their health.

 I. Coffee is addictive.

   A. Much addiction is psychological.

   B. Physical addiction can create negative symptoms.

   C. Coffee addiction is not a bad thing.

 II. Coffee consumption is associated with heart disease.

   A. Coffee may raise cholesterol.

   B. Coffee may raise blood pressure.

   C. Experts disagree about consumption rate.

   D. Experts agree about preparation process.

 III. Coffee has been connected with cancer.

   A. Older research suggests possible linkage.

   B. Recent research has not found link.

   C. Coffee may actually prevent some cancers.

 IV. Coffee does have a negative effect on unborn babies.

   A. Coffee increases danger of miscarriage.

   B. Coffee may cause low-birth-weight babies.

 V. Coffee's popularity prompts more research.

   A. Recent popularity of coffee raises old questions about health.

   B. Recent research suggests that moderate consumption is not harmful.

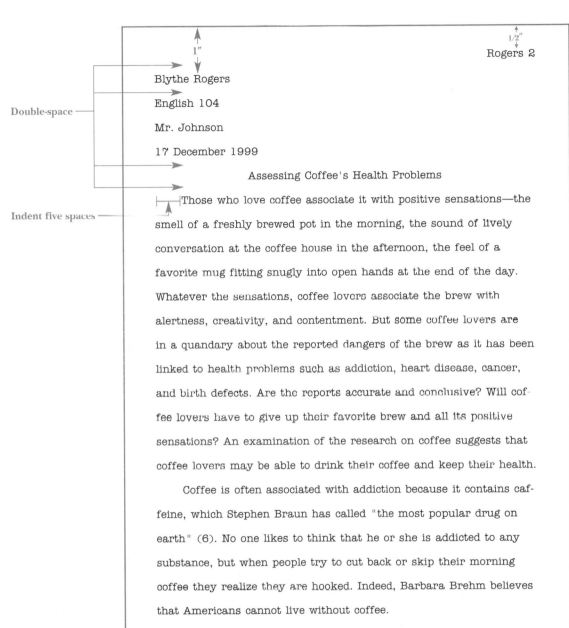

Rogers 2

Blythe Rogers

English 104

Mr. Johnson

17 December 1999

Assessing Coffee's Health Problems

Those who love coffee associate it with positive sensations—the smell of a freshly brewed pot in the morning, the sound of lively conversation at the coffee house in the afternoon, the feel of a favorite mug fitting snugly into open hands at the end of the day. Whatever the sensations, coffee lovers associate the brew with alertness, creativity, and contentment. But some coffee lovers are in a quandary about the reported dangers of the brew as it has been linked to health problems such as addiction, heart disease, cancer, and birth defects. Are the reports accurate and conclusive? Will coffee lovers have to give up their favorite brew and all its positive sensations? An examination of the research on coffee suggests that coffee lovers may be able to drink their coffee and keep their health.

Coffee is often associated with addiction because it contains caffeine, which Stephen Braun has called "the most popular drug on earth" (6). No one likes to think that he or she is addicted to any substance, but when people try to cut back or skip their morning coffee they realize they are hooked. Indeed, Barbara Brehm believes that Americans cannot live without coffee.

> Caffeine's speed-you-up effects complement American lifestyle demands. Combined with easy accessibility, caffeine addiction is a common result. Addiction is marked

Labels in left margin:
- Double-space
- Indent five spaces
- **Long quotation: A quotation of more than four lines is set off from text and is *not* placed in quotation marks.**

Margin annotations: 1", 1/2", 1"

Rogers 3

by strong psychological and physical cravings for a sub-

stance. . . . Caffeine withdrawal symptoms include

fatigue, headache, nausea and various psychological

symptoms.

Much addiction is psychological. People believe coffee stimu-

lates their senses and accelerates their thinking. Braun argues that

coffee is associated with work, "particularly work involving think-

ing, reading, writing or talking" (139). Such associations explain

why our culture has "institutionalized" the "coffee break" to help

workers regain energy and alertness (Pendergrast 241–42). But

health columnist Jane Brody explains that such positive psychologi-

cal associations do not compensate for the negative physical symp-

toms of withdrawal: "When I recently tried to give up caffeine, my

body rebelled. I developed a headache so intense that if I had not

known better I would have sworn I had a brain tumor or had suf-

fered a stroke."

Despite such horror stories, addiction does not have to become

a deadly affair like other major health concerns. As Mark

Pendergrast points put, "[a]s addictions go, [coffee] is a relatively

harmless one" (417). He cites Peter Dews, a Harvard professor, as

saying "most people are addicted to caffeine containing beverages,

just as most are addicted to showers and regular meals. That is not

a bad thing. It is a habit that can be indulged for a lifetime without

adverse effects to health" (Pendergrast 417).

Coffee is also associated with heart disease because it has been

linked with major risk factors such as high cholesterol, hypertension,

Use ellipsis points to show where you have omitted words from the original.

Short quotation: Author is identified at the beginning of the sentence as brackets are used to work quotation into the sentence.

and stress. According to Stephen Cherniske, caffeine raises blood cho-

lesterol levels and blood pressure, "increases homocysteine (a biochem-

ical that damages artery walls), promotes arrhythmia, and constricts

blood vessels leading to the heart" (5). Although not direct causes,

these problems, either alone or in combination, have a close relation-

ship to heart disease, and people who suffer from these difficulties are

warned to significantly reduce or eliminate their consumption of coffee.

Two considerations, however, must be factored into the connec-

tion between coffee and heart disease: the amount of coffee con-

sumed by the subjects in the medical study and the process by which

that coffee was prepared. Marilyn Elias argues that "a few cups of

coffee should be avoided by adults with even borderline hypertension

or a family history of heart attacks." In this same report, however,

Elias defines "a few" as more than five, and goes on to explain that

"people who consume fewer than four or five cups a day seem to

incur no cardiac risk, even if they already have clogged arteries or

irregular heart rhythms." Jane E. Brody adds to the number confu-

sion by arguing that "a significant rise in blood pressure can occur

after just two or three cups of coffee."

What most of these reports fail to mention is how coffee is pre-

pared. For example, if the coffee is unfiltered, then the correlation

between coffee consumption and cholesterol increases. A 1996

report from the Consumers Union of the United States explains that

"boiling ground coffee beans releases oils that contain two com-

pounds—cafestol and kahweol—that tend to raise levels of low

density lipoprotein (LDL) cholesterol, the artery clogging kind." If

Short quotation: Author is identified at the beginning of the sentence and quotation is worked into sentence.

Short quotation: Author is identified as an organization.

Rogers 5

the coffee is instant or drip filtered, however, the cafestol and kahweol are removed. This report suggests that such information sheds new light on the old research studies, as "nearly all the studies linking coffee with increased cholesterol have involved unfiltered coffee."

Thus, it would seem that if people consume "a few" cups of coffee and are selective about how they prepare it, they need not be alarmed about the risk of heart disease. Or to put the matter differently, if a person is truly concerned about heart disease, coffee is not the thing to worry about. They should be concerned with the more dramatic risk factors—some of which can be controlled by medicine (hypertension) and some of which can be controlled by a healthier lifestyle (obesity). For those people who already lead a healthy lifestyle, moderate consumption of coffee will not cause heart disease (James 163).

Another health concern associated with coffee is cancer. Since caffeine does alter the metabolism of the body, medical researchers have speculated that coffee might cause cancer. Like heart disease, however, cancer has multiple and indirect causes. If a person eats unhealthy food and does not consume any antioxidants, cancer might loom on the horizon. But no medical research has demonstrated a direct link between coffee and cancer. Brody reports that coffee has been associated with pancreatic cancer, breast cancer, and bladder cancer, but these were "anecdotal findings," not conclusive proof. Pendergrast reports that a 1979 "epidemiological study appeared to link coffee to pancreatic cancer, triggering widespread

Paraphrase: Source is paraphrased and the author and page are placed within parentheses.

Paraphrase: Author is identified at beginning of sentence; source is paraphrased; single-page source does not require a page number.

media attention and sick jokes about coffee being 'good to the last drop'" (340). Although the study was done twenty years ago, the negative press left its mark. People believe rumors and initial warnings and distrust the later reports that correct the findings and reassure them that it is OK to drink coffee.

Short quotation: Author and date are stated at beginning of the sentence, and ellipses are used to work source into the sentence.

In 1994, Barbara Brehm concluded that "most recent studies have not found a caffeine-cancer link. . . . And researchers no longer believe that caffeine contributes to benign breast lumps." In fact, some research shows that caffeine lowers the risk for certain cancers. Medical Data International reports that "the risk of colorectal cancer drops as the amount of coffee consumed rises." In an article in Men's Health, Matt Marion explains that "coffee increases the frequency of bowel movements, which may limit the colon's exposure to carcinogens." The plot thickens. Consumers who are told in one case to limit their coffee intake to a few cups daily are told in another case that a few cups more will help them avoid problems. No wonder coffee lovers are in a quandary.

Short quotation: Author and title of periodical establish credibility of source. A page number is not required in single-page sources.

Medical researchers do seem to agree that caffeine has a negative effect on unborn babies. Brehm advises pregnant women "to avoid caffeine [because] it may increase rates of miscarriage and low birth weight." Unborn babies "lack the liver enzyme to break down caffeine" (Pendergrast 415). In a study in Physician and Sportsmedicine, Nancy Clark summarizes these side effects:

> A woman who wants to start a family should be aware
>
> that consuming over 300 milligrams of caffeine a day

Rogers 7

might increase the time it takes to get pregnant, as well as the risk of miscarriage or a low-birth-weight baby. The U.S. Food and Drug Administration recommends that pregnant women avoid caffeine-containing foods and drugs or consume them only sparingly, because caffeine crosses the placenta and is a stimulant to the unborn baby. It is also transfered into breast milk, so women who breastfeed should avoid caffeine. (110)

No one has disproved caffeine's negative effects on the unborn. Even Pendergrast, whose positive attitude toward caffeine is often revealed in the tone of his book, agrees that pregnant women should be careful—although he does remark, lightheartedly, that coffee "turns breast milk into a kind of natural latte" (415).

In recent years, coffee has enjoyed a resurgence of popularity. Coffee lovers have become specialists in selecting designer blends and processing machinery. Coffee bars and coffee houses have become prominent features of the landscape of reality and television. This resurgence prompted medical researchers to revisit the issue of whether coffee caused health problems. But as the analysis of that research demonstrates, coffee's negative impact on health is not that severe. So coffee lovers, it would appear, need not give up their coffee or the positive sensations they associate with its consumption. If they consume coffee in moderation, coffee lovers can have their health and drink one or two cups.

Documentation: The parenthetical reference to a block quotation follows the final mark of punctuation.

Documentation: The parenthetical reference to a run-in quotation precedes the final mark of punctuation.

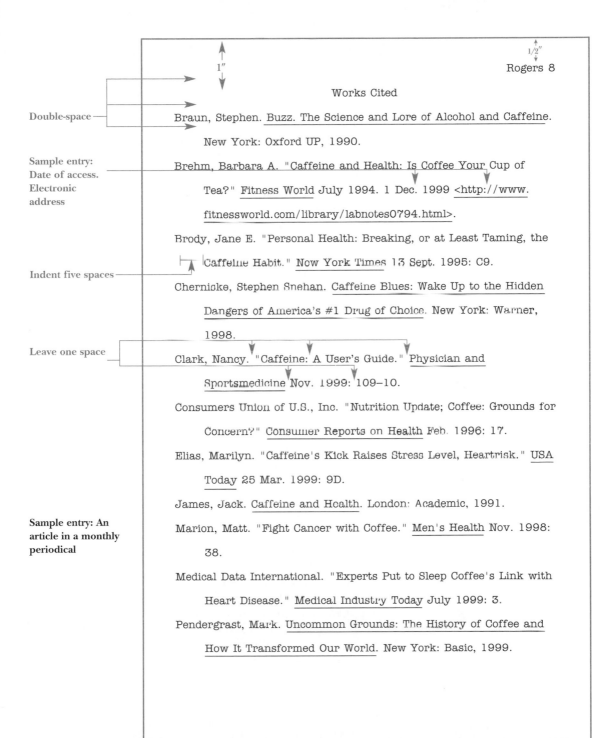

Rogers 8

Works Cited

Braun, Stephen. <u>Buzz. The Science and Lore of Alcohol and Caffeine.</u>
New York: Oxford UP, 1990.

Brehm, Barbara A. "Caffeine and Health: Is Coffee Your Cup of
Tea?" <u>Fitness World</u> July 1994. 1 Dec. 1999 <http://www.
fitnessworld.com/library/labnotes0794.html>.

Brody, Jane E. "Personal Health: Breaking, or at Least Taming, the
Caffeine Habit." <u>New York Times</u> 13 Sept. 1995: C9.

Cherniske, Stephen Snehan. <u>Caffeine Blues: Wake Up to the Hidden
Dangers of America's #1 Drug of Choice.</u> New York: Warner,
1998.

Clark, Nancy. "Caffeine: A User's Guide." <u>Physician and
Sportsmedicine</u> Nov. 1999: 109–10.

Consumers Union of U.S., Inc. "Nutrition Update; Coffee: Grounds for
Concern?" <u>Consumer Reports on Health</u> Feb. 1996: 17.

Elias, Marilyn. "Caffeine's Kick Raises Stress Level, Heartrisk." <u>USA
Today</u> 25 Mar. 1999: 9D.

James, Jack. <u>Caffeine and Health.</u> London: Academic, 1991.

Marion, Matt. "Fight Cancer with Coffee." <u>Men's Health</u> Nov. 1998:
38.

Medical Data International. "Experts Put to Sleep Coffee's Link with
Heart Disease." <u>Medical Industry Today</u> July 1999: 3.

Pendergrast, Mark. <u>Uncommon Grounds: The History of Coffee and
How It Transformed Our World.</u> New York: Basic, 1999.

(margin annotations:)
1″
½″
Double-space
Sample entry:
Date of access.
Electronic
address
Indent five spaces
Leave one space
**Sample entry: An
article in a monthly
periodical**

6. Abbreviations for MLA Documentation

Selected Publishers

When the publisher's name includes the name of one person (Harry N. Abrams, Inc.), cite the surname alone (Abrams). When the publisher's name includes the name of more than one person (Harcourt Brace), cite only the first of these names (Harcourt).

Abrams	Harry N. Abrams, Inc.
Allyn	Allyn and Bacon, Inc.
Appleton	Appleton-Century-Crofts
Basic	Basic Books
Bowker	R. R. Bowker Co.
Dodd	Dodd, Mead, and Co.
Doubleday	Doubleday and Co., Inc.
Farrar	Farrar, Straus, and Giroux, Inc.
Feminist	The Feminist Press at the City University of New York
Harcourt	Harcourt Brace
Harper	HarperCollins
Harvard UP	Harvard University Press
Holt	Holt, Rinehart and Winston, Inc.
Houghton	Houghton Mifflin Co.
Knopf	Alfred A. Knopf, Inc.
Lippincott	J. B. Lippincott Co.
MIT P	The MIT Press
MLA	The Modern Language Association of America
Norton	W. W. Norton and Co., Inc.
Oxford UP	Oxford University Press, Inc.
Princeton UP	Princeton University Press
Rand	Rand McNally and Co.
Random	Random House, Inc.
St. Martin's	St. Martin's Press, Inc.
Scribner's	Charles Scribner's Sons
Simon	Simon and Schuster, Inc.
UMI	University Microfilms International
U of Chicago P	University of Chicago Press
Viking	The Viking Press, Inc.
Yale UP	Yale University Press

Selected Reference Resources

BM	British Museum, London (now British Library)
Cong. Rec.	Congressional Record
DA, DAI	Dissertation Abstracts, Dissertation Abstracts International
DAB	Dictionary of American Biography
DNB	Dictionary of National Biography
ERIC—ED	Educational Resources Information Center— Educational Document
ERIC—EJ	Educational Resources Information Center— Educational Journal
GPO	Government Printing Office, Washington D.C.
HMSO	Her (His) Majesty's Stationery Office
LC	Library of Congress
NPR	National Public Radio
PBS	Public Broadcasting System
PC-DOS	Personal Computer-Disk Operating System

Appendix on APA Style

The purpose of documentation is twofold: (1) to avoid representing somebody else's work as your own and (2) to refer readers to the specific source you are citing. Although there is general agreement about the purpose of documentation, different fields of knowledge use different styles. If you are writing a research paper in the humanities, your instructor is likely to require MLA style. If you are writing a research paper in the social sciences, your instructor is likely to require APA (American Psychological Association) style.

In some ways, APA and MLA styles are similar. Both require an alphabetized list of sources and in-text parenthetical documentation of citations. Both use numbered notes only to convey certain kinds of information not included in the text. Some major differences between the two styles, especially APA's emphasis on date of publication, are reflected in the guidelines and illustrations given below. For further information, see the APA Publication Manual.[1]

[1]American Psychological Association, *Publication Manual of the American Psychological Association,* 5th ed. (Washington: APA, 2001).

Preparing the List of References

1. Paginate the list of sources (entitled **References**) as a continuation of your text.

2. Double-space between successive lines of an entry and between entries.

3. Begin the first line of an entry flush left, and indent successive lines three spaces.

4. List the entries in alphabetical order according to the last name of the author.

5. If you are listing more than one work by the same author, arrange the works by date of publication, starting with the earliest work. Repeat the author's name in each entry.

6. Invert the names of all authors in each entry, and use initials for the first and middle names of all authors.

7. When there is more than one author, use an ampersand (&) before the name of the last author.

8. When there are two to six authors, name all of them in the list of references. In the text, if there are three to five authors, then name all the authors the first time but abbreviate subsequent uses to only the first author followed by *et al.* (not in italics, and add a period to "al" to show that it is an abbreviation). If there are six or more authors, in the text cite only the first author followed by *et al.;* in the reference list name the first six authors and refer to the rest as *et al.*

9. Place the date of publication in parentheses immediately after the author's name. Type a period after the closing parenthesis.

10. If you list two works by the same author published in the same year, arrange the works alphabetically by title (excluding the articles *a* and *the*), and assign letters to the year to prevent confusion: (1984a), (1984b).

11. Place the article title (if any) or book title after the year of publication.

12. For books, capitalize only the first word of the book title, the first word of the book subtitle (if any), and all proper names. Underline the complete book title.

13. If the author is also the publisher of the work, put the word *Author* after the place of publication.

14. For articles in periodicals or in edited volumes, capitalize only the first word of the article title, the first word of the article subtitle (if any), and all proper names. Do not enclose the article title in quotation marks. Put a period after the article title.

15. Spell out the names of journals in upper- and lowercase letters, and underline the journal name.

16. In references to periodicals, give the volume number in arabic numerals, and underline it. Do not use *vol.* before the number.

17. Use the full name of the publisher (but omit *Publishers, Company, Inc.,* etc.).

18. In text citations, use *p.* or *pp.* for page numbers. In the reference list, use *p.* or *pp.* for newspaper pages, and omit *p.* or *pp.* for journal or magazine pages.

19. Treat inclusive page numbers in text citations and in the reference list as follows: 67–68, 102–103, 237–242, 389–421.

Sample Entries

When citing books and articles, provide the following general categories of information:

Author's last name, first initial. (Publication date). Book title. Any additional

information. City of publication: Publisher.

Author's last name, first initial. (Publication date). Article title. Periodical title,

inclusive pages.

Entries illustrating variations on this basic format appear below and are numbered to facilitate reference. To compare these entries with those documented in MLA style, refer to the page and item numbers given in brackets.

A Book by One Author

1. Light, R. J. (2001). Making the most of college: Students speak their minds.

   New York: Random House.   [3,1]

Two or More Books by the Same Author

2. Garreau, J. (1981). The nine nations of North America. Boston: Houghton

   Mifflin.   [3,3]

3. Garreau, J. (1991). Edge city: Life on the new frontier. New York:

   Doubleday.   [3,2]

A Book by Six or Fewer Authors

4. Belenky, M. F., Clichy, B. M., Goldberger, N. R., & Torule, J. M. (1986).
   Women's way of knowing: The development of self, voice, and mind.
   New York: Basic Books.   [4,6]

A Book by a Corporate Author; Author as Publisher

5. National Geographic Society. (2002). Cradle and crucible: History and faith
   in the Middle East. Washington: Author.   [4,7]

A Work in an Anthology

6. Silko, L. M. (1991). The man to send rain clouds. In W. Brown and A. Ling
   (Eds.), Imagining America: Stories from the promised land. New York:
   Persea.   [5,13]

A Signed Article from a Daily Newspaper

7. Barringer, F. (1993, March 7). Where many elderly live, signs of the
   future. The New York Times, p. 12.   [7,28]

An Article from a Weekly or Biweekly Magazine

8. Sedaris, D. (2003, March 10). Who's the chef? The New Yorker, pp. 40–41.
   [7,31]

An Article in a Journal with Continuous Pagination

9. Hesse, D. (2003). The place of creative nonfiction. College English, 65
   237–241.   [8,32]

CD-ROM: Printed Source or Printed Analogue

10. West, Cornel. (1987). The dilemma of the black intellectual. [CD–ROM].
    Critical Quarterly, 29, 39–52. From: SilverPlatter File: MLA
    International Bibliography Item: 8800011.   [9,38]

Internet Source: An Article in a Print Journal

Note how APA lists the retrieval date, that the full URL is given, and that no period follows the URL.

11. Bieder, R. A. (1996). The representation of Indian bodies in nineteenth-

century American anthropology. American Indian Quarterly, 20, 2.

Retrieved March 28, 1998, from

http://www.uoknor.edu/aiq/aiq202.html#beider   [11,46]

Documenting Sources

The following guidelines and examples show common in-text situations for the APA style of documentation.

1. When you are summarizing or paraphrasing a source and do not mention the author's name in your sentence, place the author's name and date of publication in parentheses before the sentence period. Separate each unit of information with a comma.

   Fairy tales help children explore the worlds of forbidden knowledge

   (Tuan, 1979).

2. When you are quoting and do not mention the author's name in your sentence, place the author's name, date of publication, and page number(s) in parentheses.

   Although fairy tales contain frightening information, they "thrill rather

   than terrify a healthy child" (Tuan, 1979, p. 20).

3. When you are quoting and you mention the name of the author in your sentence, place only the publication date and page number(s) in parentheses.

   Tuan (1979) suggests that the effect of fairy tales is muted by "the

   affectionate environment in which the stories are usually told" (p. 20).

4. If you use more than one source written in the same year by the same author, follow the pattern established in your reference list, and include the letter assigned to the source.

   (Turnbull, 1965b)

5. If you cite several sources in one place, list them in alphabetical order by authors' last names, and separate them with a semicolon.

The Mbuti Pygmies, carefree and harmonious, have no concept of evil and thus no real sense of fear (Tuan, 1979; Turnbull, 1965a).

References

Tuan, Y. (1979). <u>Landscapes of fear</u>. New York: Pantheon.

Turnbull, C. M. (1965a). The Mbuti Pygmies of the Congo. In J. L. Gibbs, Jr. (Ed.), <u>Peoples of Africa</u> (pp. 281–317). New York: Holt, Rinehart and Winston.

Turnbull, C. M. (1965b). <u>Wayward servants: The two worlds of the African Pygmies</u>. Garden City, NY: Natural History Press.

Index

43